How Does My Home Work?

Heating

Chris Oxlade

Heinemann
LIBRARY
Chicago, Illinois

www.capstonepub.com
Visit our website to find out more information about Heinemann-Raintree books.

To order:

☎ Phone 800-747-4992

💻 Visit www.capstonepub.com to browse our catalog and order online.

©2013 Heinemann Library
an imprint of Capstone Global Library, LLC
Chicago, Illinois

Edited by Daniel Nunn, Rebecca Rissman, and Catherine Veitch
Designed by Joanna Hinton-Malivoire
Picture research by Elizabeth Alexander
Production by Alison Parsons
Originated by Capstone Global Library Ltd
Printed and bound in China by Leo Paper Products

16 15 14 13 12
10 9 8 7 6 5 4 3 2 1

Library of Congress Cataloging-in-Publication Data
Oxlade, Chris.
  Heating / Chris Oxlade.—1st ed.
     p. cm.—(How does my home work?)
  Includes bibliographical references and index.
  ISBN 978-1-4329-6564-8 (hb)—ISBN 978-1-4329-6569-3 (pb) 1. Heat—Juvenile literature. 2. Materials—Thermal properties—Juvenile literature. 3. Change of state (Physics)—Juvenile literature. I. Title.
  QC256.O954 2013
  697—dc23   2011038247

Acknowledgments
We would like to thank the following for permission to reproduce photographs: Alamy pp. 6 (© Oleksiy Maksymenko), 9 (© Gareth Byrne), 13 (© Jon Parker Lee), 17 (© Ted Foxx), 20 (© Angela Hampton Picture Library), 21 (© PhotoAlto), glossary photo: boiler (© Gareth Byrne); Science Photo Library p. 10 (Edward Kinsman); Shutterstock p. 4 (© StockLite), 5 (© Kuznetsov Dmitriy), 7 (© Ant Clausen), 8 (© David Hughes), 11 (© vadim kozlovsky), 12 (© glennebo), 14 (© Leo Francini), 15 (© Ian Bracegirdle), 16 (© Heymo), 18 (© Georgios Alexandris), 19 (© THP | Tim Hester Photography), 23 (© THP / Tim Hester Photography, © Ant Clausen, © glennebo, © Georgios Alexandris, © David Hughes, © Heymo).

Cover photograph of a fireplace reproduced with permission of Shutterstock (© Jitloac). Background photograph of blue flames of a gas burner inside a boiler reproduced with permission of Shutterstock (© Dmitry Naumov).

Back cover photographs of (left) a gas fire reproduced with permission of Shutterstock (© Ant Clausen), and (right) insulation reproduced with permission of Shutterstock (© glennebo).

Every effort has been made to contact copyright holders of material reproduced in this book. Any omissions will be rectified in subsequent printings if notice is given to the publisher.

We would like to thank Terence Alexander for his invaluable help in the preparation of this book.

Disclaimer
All the Internet addresses (URLs) given in this book were valid at the time of going to press. However, due to the dynamic nature of the Internet, some addresses may have changed, or sites may have changed or ceased to exist since publication. While the author and Publishers regret any inconvenience this may cause readers, no responsibility for any such changes can be accepted by either the author or the Publishers.

Contents

Some words are shown in bold, **like this**. You can find them in the glossary on page 23.

What Is Heating?

fire

Heating is how we keep our homes warm when the weather is cold.

We heat our homes with heaters, **radiators**, and fires.

4

We also use heating to heat up water.

We use the hot water for washing, baths, showers, and cleaning our homes.

How Do Heaters Work?

Some heaters work using electricity.

The electricity makes the heater hot. This makes the air around the heater warm.

gas fire

Some heaters work using **fuels** such as gas, oil, coal, or wood.

The burning fuel heats the air in your home.

How Do Radiators Work?

radiator

Do not touch
a hot radiator.

Some homes have heaters called **radiators** that make them warm.

Radiators are hot because they are full of hot water.

boiler

A **boiler** burns **fuel** such as gas to heat the water.

A pump pushes the hot water through pipes to the radiators.

Will My Home Stay Warm?

When it is cold outdoors, heat from inside a home leaks out.

In this picture, the bright colors show where most of the heat is escaping.

Heat escapes quickly through open windows and doors.

We have to use more **fuel** or electricity to replace the heat that is wasted.

Can We Stop Heat from Escaping?

insulation

We stop heat from escaping from homes with material called **insulation**.

Most homes have insulation in the roof and in the walls.

double glazing

These windows have two sheets of glass in them called double glazing.

Double glazing helps to stop heat from escaping through the windows.

Where Do Fuels and Electricity Come From?

oil rig

Oil, gas, and coal are found deep under the ground.

This oil rig is getting oil from under the seabed.

Electricity is made at electricity power stations.

This power station burns coal to make electricity.

How Do We Stop Homes from Getting Too Hot?

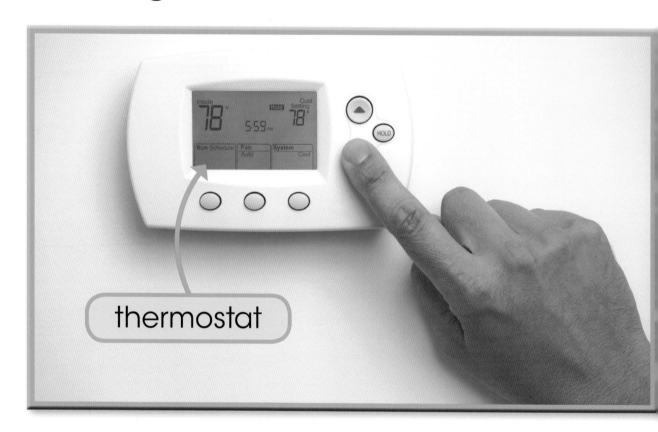

thermostat

We use a control called a **thermostat** to say how warm we want a room to be.

The thermostat turns the heater off when the room is warm enough.

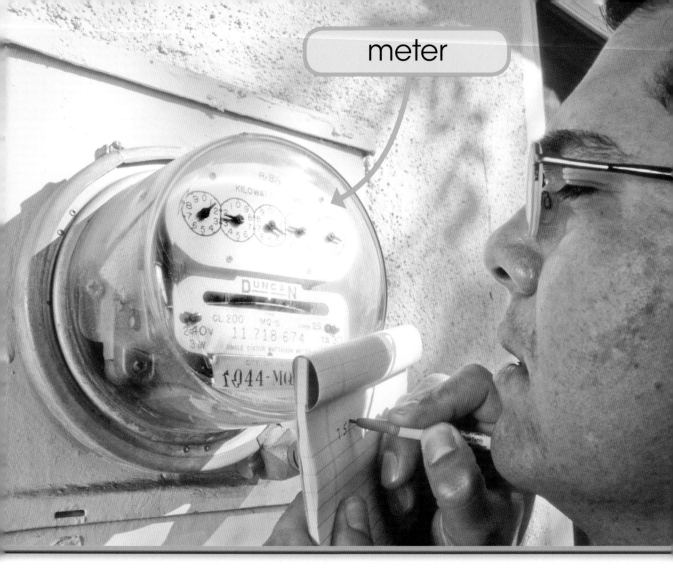

meter

Your home has an electricity meter that measures how much electricity you use.

If you turn down your thermostat a bit, you can save electricity.

Is Heating Homes Bad for Our Planet?

pollution

Burning **fuels** for heating or to make electricity makes **pollution** in the air.

Pollution is bad for our planet.

Scientists believe that burning fuels is also causing **climate change**.

Some countries may have more storms or droughts because of climate change.

How Can We Save Heat?

Turn down heating to use less **fuel** and electricity.

That will save your family money, and it helps the planet, too.

You can wear extra clothes indoors instead of turning up the heat.

Also, keep doors and windows shut in the cold weather to keep in the heat.

Saving Heat Diary

What things can you and your family do to save heat in your home?

Copy the list below. When you do one of the things on the list, put a check next to it.

Things To Do To Save Heat

- Turn down the **thermostats** on your heaters.
- Keep doors and windows closed when it is cold outside.
- Wear extra clothes instead of turning up heaters.
- Check that your home has **insulation**.
- Do not leave hot water faucets running.
- Take a shorter shower.

Glossary

 **boiler** machine that burns fuel to heat water

 **climate change** changes to the weather that happen in different parts of the world

 **fuel** material such as coal, oil, or gas that burns to give heat, light, or power

 **insulation** material that stops heat from escaping through the walls and roof of a home

 **pollution** harmful things in the air, water, or soil. It is caused by humans.

 **radiator** heater that is full of hot water. Some heaters are filled with hot oil instead.

 **thermostat** control that turns radiators or heaters on or off, depending on how hot or cold it is

Find Out More

Books

Fix, Alexandra. *Reduce, Reuse, Recycle: Energy.* Chicago: Heinemann Library, 2008.

Royston, Angela. *Protect Our Planet: Global Warming.* Chicago: Heinemann Library, 2008.

Website

www1.eere.energy.gov/kids/
Play games and learn more about saving electricity at this website.

Index